LET'S see

Cinco de Mayo

by Marc Tyler Nobleman

Content Adviser: William B. Taylor, Ph.D.,
Professor of History, University of California-Berkeley

Reading Adviser: Susan Kesselring, M.A., Literacy Educator,
Rosemount-Apple Valley-Eagan (Minnesota) School District

Let's See Library
Compass Point Books
Minneapolis, Minnesota

Compass Point Books
3109 West 50th Street, #115
Minneapolis, MN 55410

Visit Compass Point Books on the Internet at *www.compasspointbooks.com*
or e-mail your request to *custserv@compasspointbooks.com*

On the cover: Cinco de Mayo dancers in San Francisco, California

Photographs ©: Morton Beebe/Corbis, cover; Joe Raedle/Getty Images, 4; Mary Evans Picture Library, 6; Time Life Pictures/Mansell/Getty Images, 8; F. Ziglar/The Image Finders, 10; John Elk III, 12; Skjold Photographs, 14; Richard Cummins/Corbis, 16; Corel, 18; Sandy Felsenthal/Corbis, 20.

Creative Director: Terri Foley
Managing Editor: Catherine Neitge
Editor: Brenda Haugen
Photo Researcher: Marcie C. Spence
Designers: Melissa Kes and Les Tranby
Educational Consultant: Diane Smolinski

Library of Congress Cataloging-in-Publication Data
Nobleman, Marc Tyler.
  Cinco de Mayo / Marc Tyler Nobleman.
    p. cm. — (Let's see)
Includes index.
  ISBN 0-7565-0768-5 (hardcover)
1. Cinco de Mayo (Mexican holiday)—Juvenile literature. 2. Cinco de Mayo, Battle of, Puebla, Mexico, 1862—Juvenile literature. 3. Mexico—Social life and customs—Juvenile literature. 4. United States—Social life and customs—Juvenile literature. 5. Mexican Americans—Social life and customs—Juvenile literature. I. Title. II. Series.
F1233.N75 2005
394.262—dc22   2004005087

Table of Contents

What Is Cinco de Mayo? 5

What Is the Battle of Puebla? 7

What Happened After the Battle of Puebla? 9

How Is Cinco de Mayo Celebrated in Mexico? 11

How Is Cinco de Mayo Celebrated in the U.S.? 13

Who Celebrates Cinco de Mayo in the U.S.? 15

Where Is Cinco de Mayo Celebrated in the U.S.? 17

What Is Mexican Independence Day? 19

What Does Cinco de Mayo Mean to People? 21

Glossary 22

Did You Know? 22

Want to Know More? 23

Index 24

NOTE: In this book, words that are defined in the glossary
are in **bold** the first time they appear in the text.

What Is Cinco de Mayo?

Cinco de Mayo is a holiday when people remember a special time in the history of Mexico. People in the United States and Mexico celebrate this holiday.

On Cinco de Mayo, people remember how Mexicans won a big battle in 1862. It is a day when people celebrate being Mexican.

Cinco de Mayo is on May 5 every year. In Spanish, cinco de Mayo means "the fifth of May." In the United States, Cinco de Mayo is not a day off from school or work.

◄ *Children march in a parade during Cinco de Mayo festivities in Mexico.*

What Is the Battle of Puebla?

Cinco de Mayo is the **anniversary** of the Battle of Puebla. It was a fight between the Mexican army and the French army. The battle was on May 5, 1862. It happened near a Mexican town named Puebla.

This battle took place because France wanted to rule Mexico. Mexicans did not want that. The Mexican army was smaller than the French army. The Mexicans' weapons were not as good. However, the Mexicans were brave. They won the battle. This was an important **victory** for Mexico.

◄ *The French attack Puebla.*

What Happened After the Battle of Puebla?

The president of Mexico in 1862 was Benito Juárez. He said the anniversary of the Battle of Puebla would be a holiday. That holiday is called Cinco de Mayo.

Even though Mexico beat France in the Battle of Puebla, the two armies continued to fight. The French took over Mexico in 1864. Three years later, the Mexicans took their country back from the French. Since then, no other country has ruled over Mexico.

◄ Benito Juárez was elected president of Mexico in 1861.

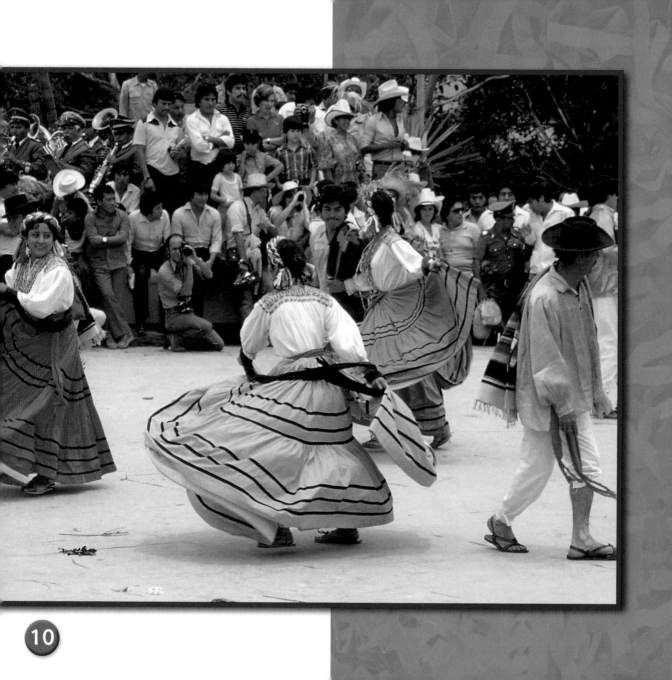

How Is Cinco de Mayo Celebrated in Mexico?

In Mexico, people dance, sing, and eat together on Cinco de Mayo. At night, they watch fireworks.

Sometimes Mexicans act out the Battle of Puebla. One group of actors plays the Mexican soldiers. Another group plays the French soldiers. People watch the actors pretend to fight. The Mexicans always win!

People celebrate Cinco de Mayo in all of Mexico. In the state and city named Puebla, Cinco de Mayo is a big event.

◄ *People dance in colorful costumes during Cinco de Mayo in Mexico.*

How Is Cinco de Mayo Celebrated in the U.S.?

Cinco de Mayo is a big event in the United States. It is a colorful, loud, and fun day.

Many people go to festivals and parades. They eat Mexican food such as tacos, enchiladas, and burritos. Some people sing or dance to Mexican music, including songs played by mariachi bands. A mariachi band is one type of Mexican band that plays **traditional** music.

Children also may play with **piñatas.** Some people shout, "Viva Mexico!" This means "long live Mexico!"

◄ *A mariachi band entertains people on Cinco de Mayo in San Antonio, Texas.*

13

ADAMS SPANISH
IMMERSION SCHOOL
ST. PAUL, MINNESOTA

Who Celebrates Cinco de Mayo in the U.S.?

People whose families came from Mexico started celebrating Cinco de Mayo in parts of the United States in the 1890s.

Today, many people in the United States celebrate Cinco de Mayo. Some are Mexicans who moved to the United States. Some are Mexican-Americans who were born in the United States and whose parents or grandparents were born in Mexico. Some people who celebrate Cinco de Mayo are not Mexican. They celebrate it because they like it. Cinco de Mayo is open to all people. It brings together Mexicans and friends of Mexicans.

◀ *Students from a school in St. Paul, Minnesota, take part in a Cinco de Mayo parade.*

Where Is Cinco de Mayo Celebrated in the U.S.?

People across the United States celebrate Cinco de Mayo. Cities in many states including California, Arizona, New Mexico, Texas, and Minnesota have Cinco de Mayo parties and carnivals.

One city that does a lot for Cinco de Mayo is Los Angeles, California. Thousands of people celebrate. They put up pictures of famous Mexicans. They wear the red, white, and green colors of the Mexican flag. Some people play guitars and other instruments in the streets. People give speeches about Mexico.

◄ *Dancers perform during the Cinco de Mayo Festival on Olvera Street in Los Angeles.*

What Is Mexican Independence Day?

Cinco de Mayo is not the same as Mexican Independence Day. They celebrate different days in Mexican history.

Cinco de Mayo is May 5. It is about the Mexican victory over the French in the Battle of Puebla. That was in 1862.

Mexican Independence Day is September 16. It celebrates a special event on that day in 1810. A Catholic priest named Miguel Hidalgo y Costilla called for Mexico's independence that day. At the time, Mexico was ruled by Spain. Mexico became independent from Spain in 1821.

◄ *The Independence Monument in Mexico City is a symbol of freedom.*

What Does Cinco de Mayo Mean to People?

On Cinco de Mayo, Mexican people show they are happy to be Mexican. They are proud their country was strong in the Battle of Puebla. They honor the people who fought for Mexico. They are **patriotic.** They celebrate their freedom.

Anyone can enjoy Cinco de Mayo. You do not have to be Mexican. Cinco de Mayo is a holiday that brings different kinds of people together.

◀ *People have fun at the Mexican Pride Parade in Chicago, Illinois.*

21

Glossary

anniversary—a date people remember because an important event took place on that day

patriotic—to show loyal support for one's country

piñatas—hollow shapes filled with candy and treats

traditional—handed down through generations of people

victory—a win

Did You Know?

* In the Battle of Puebla, the Mexican army had about 4,000 soldiers. The French army had about 6,000 soldiers.

* President Abraham Lincoln supported Mexico in the Battle of Puebla. However, he could not send troops to help Mexico because the United States was fighting the Civil War (1861–1865) at the time.

* Today, the city of Puebla is called Puebla de Zaragoza. It is named after General Ignacio Zaragoza. He led the Mexican army against the French in the Battle of Puebla. In the city, there is a museum about the battle. The museum has hundreds of toy soldiers set up to show how the battle looked. The battlefield is now a park.

Want to Know More?

At the Library

Colon Garcia, Aurora. *Cinco De Mayo.*
    Chicago: Heinemann Library, 2003.
Flanagan, Alice K. *Cinco de Mayo.*
    Minneapolis: Compass Point Books, 2004.
Gnojewski, Carol. *Cinco de Mayo:*
    Celebrating Hispanic Pride. Berkeley
    Heights, N.J.: Enslow Publishers, 2002.
Schaefer, Lola M. *Cinco de Mayo.* Mankato,
    Minn.: Pebble Books, 2001.

On the Web

For more information on *Cinco de Mayo,*
use FactHound to track down Web sites
related to this book.

1. Go to *www.facthound.com*
2. Type in a search word related to this
    book or this book ID: 0756507685.
3. Click on the *Fetch It* button.

Your trusty FactHound will fetch the best
Web sites for you!

On the Road

The Mexican Museum
Fort Mason Center
Building D
San Francisco, CA 94123
415/202-9700
To see a variety of exhibits about Mexican
and other Latino cultures

The flag of Mexico

Index

actors, 11
Battle of Puebla, 7, 9, 11, 19, 21
carnivals, 17
dance, 11, 13
date, 5
festivals, 13
food, 13
France, 7, 9, 19
Hidalgo y Costilla, Miguel, 19
Juárez, Benito, 9
Los Angeles, California, 17
mariachi bands, 13
Mexican-Americans, 15

Mexican flag, 17
Mexican Independence Day, 19
Mexico, 5, 7, 9, 11, 13, 15, 17, 19, 21
music, 13, 17
parades, 13
parties, 17
patriotism, 21
piñatas, 13
Puebla, Mexico, 7, 11
Spain, 19
speeches, 17
traditional music, 13
United States, 5, 13, 15, 17

About the Author

Marc Tyler Nobleman has written more than 40 books for young readers. He has also written for a History Channel show called "The Great American History Quiz" and for several children's magazines including *Nickelodeon*, *Highlights for Children*, and *Read* (a Weekly Reader publication). He is also a cartoonist, and his single panels have appeared in more than 100 magazines internationally. He lives in Connecticut.